Magnetic Confidence

Attract the Relationships, Results and Life You Want

By Ashley Hannawacker

www.ashleyhann.com

Magnetic Confidence

Copyright © 2018 Ashley Hannawacker

Ashley Hannawacker, Publisher

The information presented in this book is meant to supplement, not replace, proper medical advice both physical and mental. With every decision comes risk, so before performing any skills described in this book, the author and publisher advise readers to take full responsibility for their actions and safety and to know their limits.

Edited by: Pearl Edits Inc.

Copyright © 2018 Ashley Hannawacker

www.AshleyHann.com
Instagram: @ashley.hann
Facebook: @itsashleyhann
YouTube: www.youtube.com/ashleyhann

Connect with
Ashley

 Instagram: @ashley.hann

Facebook: @itsashleyhann

YouTube: @ashleyhann

Twitter: @itsashleyhann

Learn more at
www.AshleyHann.com

*I'd love to hear
from you!*

contact@ashleyhann.com

CONTENTS

DEDICATION

This book is dedicated to my amazing father and my beautiful mother.

Dad,

We've been on this self-growth journey together since I was a little girl. You've taught me courage, integrity and unconditional love. You truly are everything a daughter could wish for and more. Thank you for inspiring me every day to be the best woman I can be. I love you.

Mom,

You are my best friend and I am so incredibly grateful for our relationship. Without you, I would not be who I am today. Thank you for being there for me through everything. You are so beautiful inside and out. I love you.

This book is also dedicated to all of the women out there who are amazing, beautiful and worthy—but just don't quite know it yet. You are divine and perfectly imperfect in every way. It is my hope that this book will open your eyes to the masterpiece that you are.

A QUICK NOTE FROM ASHLEY

I'm seconds away from finishing my book and the doubt is starting to creep in. I'm scared.

That voice in my head is asking me questions.

"What if they won't like it?"

"What if I sound dumb?"

"Who am I to write a book?"

"Why would anyone want to hear my story?"

"Why would anyone want to hear what I have to say?"

"Who am I to teach magnetic confidence?"

Each question digs me further into a paralyzing, anxiety-driven hole until, finally, I just want to quit and give up.

Ever felt this way?

I feel compelled to share the vulnerable thoughts and emotions I have right now before you dive into the content of my book because we all go through this. We all have self-doubts and question our worth from time to time. Many of us experience the "imposter syndrome," get paralyzed by anxiety and feel like frauds.

It's what you *do* about it that matters.

I could easily jump ship and abandon my entire book... but I am not going to do that. It is an option I have and one that I will not take. Instead, I just close my eyes and check in with my heart, body, mind and spirit. I ask myself if I am in alignment with my truth and my purpose.

I am.

My story is my truth and sharing my message is part of my purpose. If you follow me on social media, you know I like to keep it real. I don't fake a smile and pretend everything is okay when it's not. I share my vulnerabilities because I am committed to being courageous, authentic and free to express who I am no matter what it looks like.

Yes, I get scared. Yes, I experience self-doubt. Yes, I question myself and my worthiness. And yes, I almost let these things stop me from finishing my book, pursuing my dreams and living my purpose. Many others go through the same stuff—which is why I wrote this book in the first place. My intention is not to prevent you from experiencing self-doubt; it is inevitable and part of life. The intention of my book is to inspire you to embrace and own every part of your being so that you can move through fear and attract all of your heart's desires.

I am honored that you are reading *Magnetic Confidence* and beyond grateful that I get to be a part of your journey.

It's okay to be scared, that means you're about to do something very, very brave.

— Brené Brown

INTRODUCTION

Hi beautiful! First of all, thank you for choosing to read this book. In this world of endless choices and ways to spend your time, I am so grateful to have you here with me.

The inspiration behind this book came from my own personal journey of confidence—of finding, embracing, and loving my authentic self.

If this were a self-help book cliché, I might start off by saying something like:

> *"By the end of this book, you are going to...*
>
> » *Feel more confident and be able to access your confidence whenever you need it*
>
> » *Live a happier and more fulfilled life*
>
> » *Be a walking magnet for everything you want to attract!"*

Sounds great, right? Maybe even a bit familiar? Well, I am going to get super real with you right now (and will continue to throughout this book). This is not some cliché how-to book and reading this is not going to magically transform you into a magnetically confident person.

There are too many books out there that make promises and give an illusion that change is a simple seven-step program. Change looks different for everyone and the steps I've taken and continue to take may appear very different from yours.

I do believe, however, that we can connect with, and learn from, each other's experiences and apply them to our own lives. I also know that it is entirely up to YOU to carve out the time and read this book. Not only *read* it, but really connect to the words, the feelings, and the stories. I challenge you to create your own personal breakthroughs around what you learn, participate 100%, and then practice, practice, practice by living it out in the world!

Throughout the book, I have sprinkled in chapter challenges that you absolutely *must* do. Don't just read it or skim through it and tell yourself you'll do it later, because we all know how that goes...

The time is NOW to take action!

Look—*no one can transform you.* You may receive instrumental support and guidance, but ultimately you are in charge of your journey and your results. You could have the best coach, mentor, or doctor in the world, but if you aren't willing to take action and heal, it doesn't matter how good they are. It's all about where you are and how far you are willing to go. So really, you are the author of this book. I just wrote the words for you.

Meaningful and lasting change happens when you decide to do something radically different than you've ever done. It happens when you become aware and conscious, break patterns, and step outside of your comfort zone. You must be willing to get uncomfortable. I mean, really uncomfortable. Sitting and reading about how to be confident, create change, experience transformation, and yada-yada is just that...reading about it. It's comfortable, it's easy, and it's also minimally effective.

To create real transformation and sustainable change, you must engage at a soul level. You must be willing to take the uncomfortable path and go all-in, 100%, all the way.

> To get what you haven't gotten, you need to go where you haven't been.

Growing up, my dad always repeated (and still does) Albert Einstein's famous quote, "the definition of insanity is doing the same thing over and over again, expecting different results."

You are not independent of your results. YOU are the common denominator of everything in your life. If you want something that you haven't gotten yet or to master something you haven't yet mastered, you need to be willing to get radical—to roll up your sleeves and go deep. And most importantly, *you absolutely must believe that it is possible for you to be/do/have whatever it is that you want.*

Today, people might say that I am confident, positive, outgoing, goofy, free-spirited and authentic. They may tell you that I inspired them in some way to be better, live better, and love and believe in themselves more than they ever have. They might say that I'm in great shape, love to work out, and that I am a natural on camera and speaking in front of others.

However, what most of them don't know about me is that there was a major period in my life where I had no confidence and I actually hated myself. I didn't believe. I would constantly doubt my abilities, my worth, my desires, my dreams, and even my existence. I was a prisoner of my own mind, plagued by anxiety and depression. I lived in constant fear. Fear of rejection, fear of judgement, fear of being disliked, fear of messing up, fear of failure, fear of looking dumb. I told myself I was a behind the scenes kind of girl and that I was never meant for the spotlight. I was so afraid of my light that I stayed hidden in my darkness. I lost myself there. I judged myself and everyone around me. I consistently settled for less and discounted myself. I was a girl who believed she just wasn't good enough.

Growing up, I never felt like I belonged. I wanted to be anyone else but me. I remember staring at other girls, wishing I could be more like them. Instead, I was teased and bullied. The popular girls made fun of me and threw french fries at me. I was isolated and alone. I would eat my lunch alone in the girls' bathroom stall and come home crying at least three to four times a week. I begged my mom to homeschool me. I was desperate to feel like I belonged. I started copying the ways of the popular girls and tried to fake my way into their circle. I would even make fun of myself just to be accepted by them. It was a lot of smiling and laughing on the outside while I was hurting and suffering on the inside. It was fake.

I was fake.

I would have these huge waves of depression hit me and they would last for days, sometimes even weeks. I even thought about taking my own life...more than once. I remember staring down at a handful of pills for what seemed like forever, frozen in time, imagining what dying would feel like. I thought surely it would feel better than being alive. I saw therapists and psychiatrists. I was misdiagnosed with bipolar disorder and took bipolar medication for about a year until another psychiatrist told me I actually had anxiety disorder. So, just like that, I switched to daily doses of anxiety meds. I felt like a prisoner. I was anything but free. I was trapped in a never-ending, vicious cycle of anxiety, inauthenticity, and depression that would just keep attracting more of the same into my life.

So, you want to talk about confidence? Pffft. Yeah, right. I was anything but confident.

Then, I woke up. My realization was this: *I am the main character in this sad, depressing, painful story and, here's the kicker, I am also the author. I am choosing to write this story.* Talk about mind-blowing, right? From there,

I embarked on a powerful journey of self-development and transformation. I made a commitment to always grow, but most of all, to always love myself.

Let's fast forward to today. I am 100% free from anxiety medication. I am the most free I've ever felt in my entire life. I love and accept every ounce of my being. I know my worth and own my power. I am not afraid to step into the light and be seen. I have a vision and a purpose and I stand for what I believe in...even if it means not being liked. I am a woman who sees possibility in herself and everyone around her. I have attracted the most amazing, authentic people into my life and have created an online community of amazing, beautiful women who inspire me every day. I am finally *living* my life instead of avoiding and hiding from it. I am in such gratitude to be me and to live the life that I live.

So, know this: You CAN be, do, and have anything that you want. You can stop self-doubt, self-sabotage, and fear in its tracks. You can! I know it's possible for you, because I did it. And though we may look different on the outside, you and I are the same. We are human. We are perfectly imperfect. You are not alone because I am on this journey with you—we all are.

Disclaimer: In getting to this point of self-realization and change, I did some massive, deep, intense, and committed work. I attended a four-month long self-growth and leadership training (www.ALASanDiego.com) that was extremely uncomfortable and confrontive. I rolled up my sleeves, I did the work, and I still do. Transformation and growth is constant and ever-flowing. There is no end, just lots of beautiful (and sometimes ugly) breakthroughs and new beginnings.

My number one piece of advice I can give to you is to always invest in yourself. An investment in you is a direct investment in your life, your relationships, and your results.

> *"The best investment you can make is in yourself."*
> — Warren Buffett

Magnetic Confidence

The dictionary definition of confidence is "a feeling of self-assurance arising from one's appreciation of one's own abilities or qualities." Confidence is **knowing that you are good enough.** It is the unshakable belief that you are worthy and enough.

The "magnetic" piece ties in the importance of the law of attraction. The law of attraction says that by focusing on positive or negative thoughts, a person brings a positive or negative experience into their lives. Like attracts like. This is the premise behind magnetic confidence. It ties in the law of attraction to self-belief.

> *"Our brains become magnetized with the dominant thoughts we hold in our minds...these 'magnets' attract to us the forces, the people, and the circumstances of*

life which harmonize with the nature of our dominant thoughts." —Napoleon Hill

Magnetic Confidence is the ability to attract anything and everything you want into your experience because you have the core belief and deep knowing that you are worthy of all of it. It is about being so certain of who you are and what you stand for that you essentially become like a walking magnet, attracting everything that you authentically desire into your life. This is the #MagneticMovement.

To be magnetically confident, you must...

» Believe in your worth. Know that you are worthy, capable, and enough.

» Love and accept yourself and everyone around you.

» Be brave! Face your fears and be willing to get uncomfortable.

» Be unconditionally authentic and stay true to yourself no matter what.

» Be present and connected. Be fully in the here and now.

» Own it ALL and take responsibility for your life and everything and everyone in it (including the bad stuff).

» Shake it off and be able to shift your mood or mindset when it is not serving you.

We are going to dive into each one of these and discuss what they truly mean and how you can master each of them. Now, let's take the journey to magnetic confidence.

You will attract & receive
what you believe
you are worthy of
attracting and receiving.
Period.

THOUGHTS & BELIEFS

"Your beliefs become your thoughts,
Your thoughts become your words,
Your words become your actions,
Your actions become your habits,
Your habits become your values,
Your values become your destiny."
—Mahatma Gandhi

My dad had a version of this quote plastered all over our house growing up. He taught me at a young age how important my thoughts and beliefs are. Our thoughts and beliefs are everything. They can expand us just as much as they can limit us. They can be attractive or repulsive. We must be super mindful and consciously aware of everything we think and believe. I cannot stress this enough. The main reason to be wary of this is that the principle of magnetism and attraction does not discriminate between constructive and destructive thoughts. It will translate whatever thought you have, be it good or bad, into existence.

"The law of attraction doesn't care whether you perceive something to be good or bad or whether you don't want it or you do want it, it's responding to your thoughts." —Bob Doyle

Our belief system is the lens through which we view and interpret life. You can think of it as a filter through which incoming information is processed. Most researchers agree that by age six, a person's belief system is fairly well formed.[1] From the time we are born, our sensory experiences (what we see, smell, hear, feel, taste, etc.) are used to make sense of our world. These experiences and memories birth our core beliefs, which guide our thinking, decisions and ultimately, our behaviors.

What this also means is if we had an experience early on that was even slightly traumatic, it is likely that we formed some sort of belief around that experience to protect ourselves from ever having to experience it again. It could be something as simple as you sharing a secret with your best friend and she goes and tells everyone behind your back. The belief one could create from this experience is "people cannot be trusted" and the behavior that results is you do not allow yourself to get close or truly open up to others because of the fear that they might betray you. I like to call such ideas "limiting beliefs." I also like to call them the "self-sabotaging stories" we tell ourselves that greatly limit us in our lives. In order to be magnetically confident, it is absolutely crucial that we identify, confront, deconstruct, and replace these limiting beliefs that are robbing us of our true capacity and possibilities in life.

Limiting Beliefs

The best way I've found to identify all of my limiting beliefs is to find all of the areas in my life that I am not 100% happy with or find myself struggling in. Once I identify these places where I experience trouble, I go through each area one by one and pay close attention to the initial thoughts that make their way into my consciousness. It's especially helpful if you do this as a form of meditation. Sitting in stillness and being super present and in the moment are very supportive in going deep and bringing these core beliefs up to the surface so that you can see them clearly.

For example, one of the areas I found myself really struggling with was my social life. I had severe social anxiety and found it really hard to be in social settings and groups of people. It was uncomfortable for me and I found it very difficult to introduce myself to others and start conversations. When I sat with this and allowed all of the thoughts and feelings to come up, I realized one of my limiting beliefs was that no one would want to be friends with me. It was a fear of rejection.

You know what's crazy? This belief became my reality. I believed I was going to be rejected and so I was. No one tried to be friends with me. However, it wasn't because I wasn't cool, attractive, or fun to be around; it's because I didn't believe I was. We are energetic beings. We are constantly emitting energetic vibrations out into our universe without even realizing we are doing it. People around us feel our energy and they react and respond to it. Have you ever met someone and right away, even though you know barely anything about them, you feel a sense of confidence in them? Whether it be personally or professionally, you think "Ah, this is someone I want in my life." Well, that is all energy, guys. And guess where it started from? The confidence and belief they have in themselves. The belief that they are capable and worthy has you also believing that they are. Any strong, core belief you have will manifest and create a parallel reality. Let me put it simply: your core beliefs create your reality. This is the part about limiting beliefs that you must understand. So, if you want more friends and acceptance, for example, you must accept yourself first. You must believe you are worthy of friendship and that you are an incredible, one-of-a-kind friend. You've got to be asking yourself questions like, "Who wouldn't want to be my friend? I'm f*cking amazing!" **You must believe it to see it, not the other way around.** As a mentor of mine once said, "If you don't believe in yourself, who will?"

In Dr. Lipton's book *The Biology of Belief*, he explains that when we change our beliefs, we can actually change our biochemistry and can even impact our genes. Through his research, he has found that our biochemistry and genes are influenced by our thoughts and emotions.[1] Crazy, right?

Women are particularly vulnerable to the hurtful and false belief that they don't deserve to be loved. If, as a child, you witnessed abuse or were directly abused, you may be even more prone to this belief. For many of us who carry this belief, we do so unconsciously. It is hidden in our subconscious and it can generate a lot of fear and self-sabotage. When we feel unworthy of love, it is very hard for us to determine our own worth and we end up placing it in other people and external things. We also tend to project these unworthy feelings onto others and thereby sabotage any chance of us actually experiencing love.

Worthiness

Feelings of unworthiness can be extremely self-destructive and will keep us from creating the life we desire. I truly believe that worthiness lies at the heart of achieving not just confidence, but achievement itself. This is not about other people deeming you as worthy, but about you having the deep knowing that you are worthy. You must not rely on any outside source to make you feel worthy or complete. Depending on others or external sources for worthiness, happiness, joy or fulfillment is risky and it does not work. This is because you cannot directly control what is outside of you, but you can 100% control what is inside of you and what you choose to radiate out into the world.

Worthiness comes from within and it is unconditional. It cannot be proven or disproven because it resides at the core of your being. There is nothing you can do, say, or possess to be more or less worthy. So many of us try to prove our worth by doing or obtaining things. All this does is keep us in the space of experiencing unworthiness because in order to even be on the quest of proving your worth, you must first have the belief that you are unworthy to begin with. In trying to prove your worth, you are really running from your fear of being unworthy, which puts you in a vicious cycle.

Worthiness is my journey. For a long time, I was trapped in a vicious cycle, a self-perpetuating reality that I was creating for myself based on the belief that I was not worthy. I would discount my worth in relationships and in business. Many opportunities would present themselves in my life, but I either wouldn't see them or would sabotage them out of fear that I wasn't worthy. I consistently doubted myself and my worth. I even had doubts arise while writing this book. *Who am I to be writing this book? Why should anyone listen to me?* These thoughts never go away, they just impact you less and less the more aware you become of them and the more you believe in and own your true worth. Now, I know better than to let that scared little voice in my head stop me from pursuing my dreams and my vision.

When you realize that you are truly worthy of love, you open the door to start receiving it. When you realize you are truly worth of respect, you will start getting it. If you are currently in a relationship where you are consistently being disrespected and mistreated, ask yourself why you are allowing it to continue. Deep down, there is a lack of self-worth and self-respect that is permitting and attracting this kind of relationship. Someone can only love and respect you as much as you love and respect yourself.

You will attract and receive what you believe you are worthy of attracting and receiving. Period.

Internal worthiness is directly tied to prosperity and wealth. When you learn how much you are worth, you will stop giving people discounts. And when you truly believe you are worthy of making X amount of money, you will make it. I remember when I started charging double what I used to charge my clients. It was a crazy awakening for me. The only reason I was able to close deals and charge more is because I truly believed I was worth the amount I was charging. By the same token, the only time I didn't close deals was when I was experiencing self-doubt and unworthiness. Feeling worthy takes work. It is a daily practice and a life-long journey. As long as you choose to walk the worthiness path, you will continue to realize your ever-budding worth.

Now I know better than to discount myself or what I do. I know that I am the best of the best at creating premium, high-converting websites, branding, copywriting, and strategy consulting. I charge five times what I used to charge and my clients are ten times happier. Why? Because when you actually start really believing and investing in yourself, that's when the magic happens. You'll blow your mind with how truly amazing and gifted you are. Crazy how that works, right?

An incredibly gifted love coach I know was having a really tough time closing clients. She would try different price points based on research and advice she was given, but wasn't experiencing much success. Finally, I asked her point-blank, "What do *you* feel good about charging? What feels like an *easy* price-point to close?" She said her answer without hesitation. She was certain she could charge that much for what she does. And *boom*, just like that, the same day (just hours later) she closed a client at that exact rate. This is a prime example of receiving and attaining what we believe we are worthy of. Just imagine the possibilities. What if you truly believed you were worthy of exactly what it is that you deeply desire? I'd bet my bottom dollar it would happen.

Prioritize Yourself

> *"Prioritize your mental, emotional, spiritual, and physical well-being. Self-care is a vital part of your personal growth."* —Ruben Chavez

Everything in YOUR life starts and ends with YOU. Taking care of yourself is taking care of everything in your life, including others. Many of us struggle with the idea of putting ourselves first and we have the misconception that prioritizing ourselves is selfish when, in reality, it is quite the opposite. The fact is, you can't pour from an empty cup and you aren't doing anyone any good if you are showing up run-down, stressed-out, and just a big hot-mess-and-a-half. Just as the famous airline saying goes, "Put on your own oxygen mask first before assisting others." The way you show up matters, and you won't be able to help anyone if you are showing up with an empty oxygen tank.

Magnetic confidence is all about belief-based attraction. So, think about it this way: if you are not seeing yourself as a worthwhile priority, how do you expect others to view and treat you this way? If you are not taking care of yourself and prioritizing your health and happiness, imagine the kinds of relationships you could be attracting into your life.

The most common reasons I hear for not prioritizing self-care is, "I'm too busy," or "I don't have enough time." However, what many of us don't realize is that we teach others how to treat us by our own actions and attitudes toward ourselves. So, if you are too busy or don't have enough time for yourself, you could be attracting people who take advantage of your time and good nature. You could be creating your own self-fulfilling prophecy without even realizing it.

What it really boils down to again is self-worth. By not making ourselves a priority, we are acting on the underlying belief that others are worth more than we are. If we are truly confident in who we are, love ourselves wholly, and see ourselves as worthy, then that is exactly what we will attract back. The key to healthy, meaningful relationships is to love ourselves first.

So, what does self-care look like? Well, contrary to popular belief it isn't just getting your hair and nails done (although it can certainly include that). True self-care happens when you do something that lights you up from your core. It's something you do for yourself that while you're doing it or when you're done, makes you feel vibrant and full of life. You go from being worn-down, exhausted, and grim to energetic, lively, and radiant. It is different for every person and it is important to honor what is authentic to you and not just what other people say self-care is.

For me, my top ten acts of self-care are when I commit to:

1. My health and exercising regularly
2. Reading, learning, and challenging myself
3. Being fully in and embracing the present moment
4. Setting healthy boundaries and honoring them by saying no when I need to
5. Experiencing gratitude and focusing on what I am grateful for
6. Singing and dancing to whatever kind of music suits my mood
7. Maintaining my favorite feminine features: nails, hair, skin
8. Getting massages
9. Getting a full night of uninterrupted, delicious beauty sleep
10. Being and cherishing my authentic self and trusting my intuition

The key to owning and radiating magnetic self-confidence is knowing you are worthy of being prioritized, loved, and respected. Know this: you are a queen. You are royalty, you are important, and you matter. Treat yourself as such.

Chapter Challenge:
Self-Care

*Write out a list of at least ten acts of self-care that really fill you up and speak to your soul. **Bonus points if you can think of twenty.

*Make a genuine commitment to yourself to do at least ONE of your self-care practices every day AND to indulge in a bigger one at least once a week.

*A great way to do this is to create a daily ritual. Better yet, you can create multiple daily rituals that fill your cup throughout the day. For example, my morning ritual that I look forward to every single day is waking up, slipping into my cozy robe, making a fresh cup of coffee, lighting my favorite scented candles, playing my favorite soft, instrumental morning music, and reading my book with my feet propped up on the couch for twenty to thirty minutes. I am very passionate about this ritual and I do it no matter what, even if I'm travelling, on vacation, or have an extremely busy day ahead. ;) #NoExcuses

You are
the projector
for the movie
screen that is
your life.

PERCEPTION & PROJECTION

"When you change the way you look at things, the things you look at change." —Wayne Dyer

The way we see and interpret the world around us is our perception. The dictionary definition of perception is "a way of regarding, understanding, or interpreting something; a mental impression." Beliefs are essentially the guideposts to our perception and how we choose to view the world, events, and people around us.

When you have magnetic confidence, you are aware and conscious of not just your perception, but the perception of others. You are present to your internal dialogue and the external dialogue around you. You are aware that there are more perceptions than just your own and that there is no right or wrong way because right vs. wrong is just a personal judgement. You respect and honor the perceptions of others. You also realize that your beliefs and perceptions can be projected onto others.

During the four-month self-development and emotional intelligence program I attended called Ascension Leadership Academy in San Diego, I received some powerful feedback about the way that I was showing up that really shocked me. I discovered that the way I showed up was stuck up and holier-than-thou, which was the exact opposite of how I felt at the time. What I realized is that I was projecting my unworthiness onto other people, essentially making them feel that they were not worthy enough to talk to me. I was projecting my fears onto them and making my own fears come to life by doing so. I was unapproachable because I feared I was not worthy of being approached. Crazy, right?

You are the projector for the movie screen that is your life. You decide how to view and interpret every person, event, object, situation, and circumstance. You are the creator of your own reality. What exists inside of you is what will exist outside of you. Yep, you really are that powerful. Think about it. Have you ever noticed that when you feel uncomfortable, sometimes you end up making the person or people you are with uncomfortable? It's like that saying goes, "It's only awkward if you make it awkward." How you choose to interpret each person and situation is a decision you make either consciously or unconsciously and it will dictate and command the energy you are creating and attracting in that moment.

One of my good friends used to frequently say, "There are no attractive, decent men my age in this city." Mind you, she lives in a city with a population of over 100,000 and is surrounded by several large neighboring cities. This is what I like to call a "sabotaging belief" because it is sabotaging what she actually wants and desires: to find attractive, decent men her age.

> *"Whatever you focus on is what you get."*
> —Tony Robbins

This was her perception, which became her projection and ultimately, her reality. You see what you choose to see and you will *always* find proof for your perception. You will begin to build a case supporting your belief, even though it is not actually true or even rational in most cases.

We are energetic beings. The stronger our energy is, the more contagious it is. This is why human interactions are like mirrors. We are mirroring the person we are interacting with and they are mirroring us. We are projecting and reflecting each other in many different ways, some more obvious than others. This is why it is so important to create a tribe of people around you that carry a high vibration and an energy that is in alignment with who you are and aspire to be.

It all starts with a single thought. This is why it is so important to be mindful and aware of your thoughts. Of course you will have limiting and negative thoughts; you are only human. However, you have the freedom to choose which thoughts you actually want to give energy to and which thoughts you don't and want to let go of. It takes practice, but just like anything else, the more you do it, the easier it gets. The first step is always *awareness*. When you think a thought that does not serve you or your mission, let it go and choose a thought that moves you forward.

The Power of Language

What you say matters. The minute you speak a thought out loud, you give power to it. Being mindful of what comes out of your mouth is important in manifesting and attracting the results you want in your life.

Being in online fitness, a very common goal I hear all too often is to lose weight. Well, first off, if you want to lose weight, don't you *ever* catch me hearing you say, "It's hard for me to lose weight." I don't care what your experience has been. Do not say such self-defeating and self-sabotaging nonsense out loud. Before you say anything, always ask yourself: *will what I am about to say forward me? Will it inspire me get to where I want to go? Does it feel good to say?* If the answer is no or if you even hesitate and have to think about the answer, don't say it.

So, let's find and replace the negatively-charged words in the statement "It is hard for me to lose weight." The word "hard" is an obvious negative as it is self-defeating in your quest to reach your goal. The second negatively charged word that may surprise you is the word "lose." To lose something means you are being deprived of or suffering the loss of something. Well, we all know that ain't true. A much more empowering word would be to "release" weight, instead of lose it. To release means to set free or allow something to move, act, or flow freely. Ahh, that feels much better right? So, let's rewrite this sentence shall we? Let's replace "hard" with "easy" and "lose" with "release."

It is ~~hard~~ easy for me to ~~lose~~
release weight.

Yes. It is easy to release the weight that is no longer serving you. As Jenna Phillips, public speaker, unicorn and Founder of Unicorn University and ALA San Diego says, "Embrace it, love it, and let it go." Love your body and your body will love you back. It is so important to be in harmony with your body, as well as your food choices.

If you are not sure whether what you are thinking or saying is self-sabotaging, pay close attention to your language and word choice. There are certain words and phrases that are very low vibrating and self-deprecating in nature and using them will rob you of your confidence and sabotage your goals. Pay attention to the feeling in your body when you say certain words and phrases. Do you feel powerful or weak? Empowered or defeated? Nine times out of ten, your body will answer for you if you just take a second to tap and tune in.

To get you started on the path of using powerful, empowering language, I have created a list of the top six words and phrases to absolutely stay away from. Eliminating these from your vocabulary will get you started on the path to reprogramming your thoughts, communication, and vibration so that you can manifest and attract your goals and desires.

1. **"Can't"**

   This is probably the most obvious word and I hear people using it every day. It carries such a negative charge and completely sabotages your possibilities. In the famous words of Henry Ford, "Whether you think you can or you think you can't—you're right."

2. **"Should"**

   This word is full of judgement and shame. It induces guilt and can be very disempowering. Instead, replace this word with "would like to" or "could." *Stop should-ing on yourself and other people.*

3. **"Hope"**

   This word is tricky because there are times when it is appropriate, wishing someone well, for example. However, when it comes to your personal goals and desires, hope implies that you don't trust yourself to get there and that it is out of your control. It is what I like to call a "back-door word" because it leaves a back-door open to any goal or declaration you have just in case it doesn't come to fruition. What you don't realize is what you are already manifesting in that moment is the possibility that it won't work out. You are giving yourself a back-door because of fear of failure. Trust yourself and know that failing and messing up is what makes us human and there is nothing wrong with it.

4. **"Have to"**

First off, you don't "have to" do anything. Everything is a choice. This phrase not only takes away your freedom, it is also a total joy-killer. Notice the energy you feel when you use the phrase "I have to." It is very low-vibrating and has a feeling of *dread* associated with it. A phrase to replace it with is "get to." Even if it is something as crazy-sounding as, "I get to clean my house." The reason I love this so much more is because it is a total gratitude-check. Yes, I am blessed to clean my house because I am fortunate enough to have a house to clean. Gratitude is one of the most powerful ways to shift out of any negative feeling and enter a state of bliss and joy.

5. **"Try"**

This is another back-door word. As the famous line goes, "Do or do not. There is no try." When you use this word in relation to your goals or desires, you are instantly undercutting your ability to achieve them.

6. **"But"**

This is one that I am very actively working on eliminating from my vocabulary. When you use the word "but," you are instantly negating whatever was just said in the previous sentence. One of my good friends and author of the book

Sticky Affirmations, Amber Valdez, once told me that using this word when conversing with other people can leave them not feeling heard or respected. This is something I hadn't really put much thought into before. For example, you may be having a disagreement with someone and in the back and forth debate you manage to blurt out "Yeah, but..." right after they finish their sentence. In that moment, you are replacing what they just said with what you are about to say. Instead, even if you don't agree with what they just said, say "Yes, *and..*" when it's your turn to speak. This respects the other person's perspective and lets them know you are hearing them AND that you also have an opinion about the situation. It's a win-win instead of a win-lose.

Chapter Challenge:
Rewrite Your Stories

**This is one of my all-time favorite activities so please, don't just read this activity and do nothing. Don't say you'll do it later. Do it now. The time is NOW and now is not the time to be lazy!

*Grab a pen and paper and go somewhere you can sit and be still with no distractions. If you're somewhere loud, put on some headphones and listen to some soothing instrumental music.

*Think of 1-3 areas in your life you wish to improve or that you are not happy with. Write them down.

*Meditate on each of these areas (one at a time) and write down any limiting beliefs that pop up around them that could be sabotaging you from reaching your goal.

*Now, for the best part: we are going to rewrite your stories, girl! After you have finished going through each area and writing down all of the limiting beliefs that come up, look at each of them and think of what the opposites are.

*Cross out the old icky-feeling, self-sabotaging stories and write down your new, good-feeling, self-affirming stories. Here's an example:

~~I am not smart enough.~~ → *I am brilliant! I am smart. I am more than capable. I am so good at what I do!*

*Go write these new self-affirming stories on a sticky note and put them somewhere where you can see them and be reminded every day of how amazing and worthy you are. I've also seen people put them on their phone as recurring daily reminders. I really recommend saying them out loud daily, maybe as part of your morning ritual or daily meditation. It's one thing to think a thought, but speaking it out into the universe gives it even more manifestation power.

*The great part about this exercise is that you can do it again and again. You can use it for anything, not just goals. For example, any time you are faced with any anxiety or fear you can confront the sabotaging stories that are at play and replace them with ones that boost your confidence and set you up for success. This is a very powerful practice that can drive very powerful results.

Find a why that makes you cry.

ACHIEVING GOALS & RESULTS

"In order to succeed, your desire for success should be greater than your fear of failure." —Bill Cosby

As we discussed in the previous chapter, self-belief is absolutely mandatory for having confidence and attracting whatever it is that you want; believing is seeing. Now, while your beliefs are the baseboard to achievement, there are some additional factors that play a huge role in your success.

To attract the results that you want, you must be specific about what it is you want to achieve and you must have a deep, burning desire to fuel it. Your burning desire is what will drive you to wherever you want to go, no matter what obstacles show up in your path. No one, no thing, and no circumstance or situation could ever deter you from your mission. Challenges and unexpected detours will show up—that's life. The way you react and respond to whatever is thrown your way in life is up to you. Your burning desire must be BIGGER than your darkest fears. So, how do you get this "burning desire" I so speak of? You discover and connect with your WHY. Your why is your purpose.

Why do you want it? Why is it so important to you? What is *your why*?

You can think of your purpose as the match and your burning desire as the candle flame. Your why is what lights a fire in your soul and creates the incessant, burning desire that will manifest miracles in your life. It all starts with your purpose. It cannot be just any purpose though. A surface purpose will not work. Something like, "I want to make seven figures" or "I want to fit in my size three jeans" may sound totally awesome on the surface, and it may even fuel you for a little while, but it is not going to last. It is not sustainable. This is why so many people rubber band on their goals; they lose weight to fit in a wedding dress only to gain it right back after the honeymoon. A surface purpose will only get you so far. If you want to ignite a relentless, burning desire in your soul, you've got to have a deep purpose that affects you to your core; *a why that makes you cry*.

Whenever I share my why, I cry almost every time. My eyes are filled with tears right now as I am writing this, just thinking about it.

My purpose and mission on this planet is to inspire every woman to fall deeply in love with herself, to embrace who she authentically is and all of the beautiful gifts she has, and to know that she truly matters and is worthy of everything her heart desires.

If I can connect with her heart and speak to her soul in such a way that leaves her feeling inspired and empowered to own her worth and love and cherish herself as the divine, unrepeatable miracle that she is...I've done it. I've fulfilled my purpose.

And the best part is every time you fulfill your purpose, your flame burns even brighter. This is why they say the gift is in the giving; because when you give from your heart, you receive the biggest, brightest blessings.

So when you uncover your why, hold on to it. Write it down and look at it at least once every week. On the road to achieving your goals, you must constantly reconnect with your purpose to keep the flame of your burning desire lit. Sometimes life can get a little crazy and, in the hustle and bustle of day-to-day living, we may start to forget our why. Don't let this happen to you. Do whatever it takes to keep that fire burning, sister.

Visualization & Feeling

One of the most powerful ways to attract and manifest results, relationships, and the life that you want is to visualize yourself having them. Visualization is a powerful manifestation technique that can be used to turn any goal into a reality. To take it a step further, there is a crucial, less discussed component of the creative visualization process that plays a major role in attracting your goals and desires: *using your feelings and emotions.* You must learn to feel what it would feel like had you already achieved your intended outcome in the present moment. Where imagination is the engine of your thoughts, your feelings are the fuel. Emotions are energy in motion. They are alive and they vibrate at great frequencies. The manifestation power of any mental image is determined by the frequency at which it is vibrating, the strength of not just the image itself, but of the feelings and emotions associated with it. I love these two quotes by Neville Goddard from his book *Feeling is the Secret*:

> *"Ideas are impressed on the subconscious through the medium of feeling. No idea can be impressed on the subconscious until it is felt, but once felt – be it good, bad, or indifferent – it must be expressed. Feeling is the one and only medium through which ideas are conveyed to the subconscious. Therefore, the man who does not control his feeling may easily impress the subconscious with undesirable states. By control of feeling is not meant restraint or suppression of your feeling, but rather the disciplining of self to imagine and entertain only such feeling as contributes to your happiness. Control of your feeling is all important to a full and happy life.*

> *All you can possibly need or desire is already yours. You need no helper to give it to you; it is yours now. Call*

> *your desires into being by imagining and feeling your wish fulfilled."*

Imagine yourself exactly where you want to be or with what you want to have. Close your eyes and imagine as if you have already achieved it. Harness whatever feelings naturally begin to arise. Maybe it's a feeling of excitement or peace or love or joy. Whatever it is, hold on to that feeling so that you can impress it in your subconscious.

> ...Don't stop belieeevin'! Hold on to that feeeeeelin'! Streetlight! People!

Sorry...I had to. Anyway, let's recap on the steps to becoming a magnet for attracting results and turning all of your goals into a reality.

1. Start with the belief in yourself and your worthiness of achievement.

2. Set a definite goal or specific result that you want.

3. Uncover your why that makes you cry! Identify your true purpose behind the goal.

4. Ignite the fire; allow yourself to experience the burning desire to reach your goal.

5. Visualize yourself as having achieved the goal and feel it in your body; feel all of the emotions and feelings that are associated with it.

You are perfectly imperfect. A divine masterpiece.

LOVE & ACCEPTANCE

"I will love the light for it shows me the way, yet I will endure the darkness because it shows me the stars."
—Og Mandino

A magnetically confident woman is loving and accepting of herself and of others. She is kind and compassionate. She does not reject or criticize. She embraces and celebrates. She is open and connected. She does not resist or restrain herself. She is raw and shameless and inspires others to be the same.

Perfectionism

So many of us strive to be perfect and fit certain societal standards portrayed in the media that are flawed to begin with. The fact is: no one is perfect. No one. No one is better than you, worse than you, or less than you. Those are purely judgments and are completely subjective.

What is better to one person might be quite the opposite to another. So my point is this: why go there? Why put yourself or others down? Why choose a judgement that puts you in a place of self-beat-up or leaves you feeling less-than or upset and sad? You must realize that how you view yourself and others is 100% your choice. If you want to view yourself as less than another or as being this flawed individual that can't do anything right or isn't enough, then my question to you is: why? Why look at yourself through such a condemning, harsh lens? Through decades of research, doctors have found that perfectionism correlates with depression, anxiety, eating disorders and other mental health issues.[2]

Quit striving to be perfect. Perfection is an unachievable goal because it relies completely on perception. We want to be perceived as perfect by others. The underlying issue with that is everyone's idea of perfection is different and we simply cannot control someone else's perception, no matter how hard we try. It just won't work. This is why it is so important to practice being loving and compassionate with ourselves so that we can embrace our imperfections and love ourselves wholly and completely. Our imperfections are not inadequacies; they are reminders that we are human and that we are not alone. Resisting our imperfections will leave us feeling isolated, while embracing these human parts of us will have us feeling whole and connected.

I remember when I used to hide out and play lone-wolf whenever I was in a dark place. I was ashamed and didn't want others to think less of me, so I wouldn't allow myself to be seen going through those darker moments in my life. When people hide out, numb out, or act out, it is usually because there is some inner darkness or hurt going on that they are resisting or embarrassed of. They are judging themselves and thereby projecting their judgment fears onto others.

Listen, we are all human. We all have a mixture of light and darkness within us. There are parts about us that we are happy with and parts that we may want to change or improve...and that is OKAY. However, when you dislike or reject a certain aspect of yourself, you are in a state of resistance. Remember the quote by Carl Jung? "What you resist, persists." The more you resist it, the more it festers and grows. You must embrace and accept it, especially if you want to transform and transcend it. Be as compassionate with yourself as you would with someone that you love and care about deeply.

> When you embrace your imperfections, you create a deeper connection with yourself and with others.

Think about a time when someone vulnerably shared a difficult time they were having with you. In that moment, I'll bet you felt a deeper bond with that person. Your level of love, trust, and respect for that person also probably grew. When people are courageous enough to express themselves vulnerably and brave enough to allow themselves to be seen just as they are, THAT is attractive. Not only is it attractive, but it also creates instant intimacy and connection. Why? Because every single person on this planet has one thing in common:

we are all human. Even if someone cannot relate to your specific experience, they will likely relate to the human emotions and feelings that are connected to it.

So, quit acting like a robot. Ain't nobody got time for robots. When someone asks you if you are okay and you are not okay, answer honestly and openly. Sometimes it is OKAY to not be OKAY. No one is happy all of the time. Everyone experiences darkness. Trying to be perfect 100% of the time is not just unrealistic, it's also exhausting and unattractive. The next time you are going through a raw, human moment—don't resist or hide it. Let yourself be seen, let people in, and share what you are going through. Own it. Embrace your dark moments and use them as a platform for connection and growth. After all, the only way to overcome your darkness is to shine light on it. There is nothing more magnetic and attractive than a woman who owns the beauty in her contrast. It draws people in and gives them permission to do the same.

There is also nothing sexier than a woman who owns every intricate, imperfect detail of her body; from the little wrinkles that form around her eyes when she laughs to the way her body curves. Forget airbrushing and manipulating your photos, ladies. That is NOT sexy. Own who you are, wholly and completely. Don't cake on a bunch of makeup or use makeup as a mask that you then depend on to make you feel confident. Truth be told, I love makeup—it is super fun to play with and I believe it is a great way to accentuate your best features. However, what we don't want is to create an unhealthy relationship with it or use it to hide who we are.

A couple of months ago I took a trip back to my hometown near Seattle to visit my family. Well, I must have been in a bit of a rush when I packed because when I arrived at my dad's house and unpacked my suitcase, I noticed something very important was missing—my entire makeup bag. At first, I got upset and then I began to laugh. Clearly, I had never forgotten to pack my makeup before and I found my initial reaction to be pretty humorous. "Oh no! What am I going to do?" How about not wear my makeup for the next week? I went from feeling distraught to laughing to a bit relieved and excited within a matter of seconds.

Use things like makeup, clothes, jewelry, etc. as a way to *accentuate* who you are, not define who you are. Wear outfits and style yourself in a way that makes you feel good. Use it as a form of self-expression. What matters most is that you wear clothing that is true to who you are and makes you feel sexy, vibrant, and confident. It's about having what you feel or want to feel on the inside match your outside. Rely on who you are, not what you wear, to make you magnetically confident! You are either as beautiful or as ugly as you believe you are. Beauty is perception—you define it. It is not a power that anyone else can have over you.

I had an interesting conversation the other day with one of my soul sisters, Julie Serot, who is an incredible business coach, teaching women the magic of manifesting miracles in their businesses. We talked about the beauty of choice and contrast. In every moment of our lives, we have the choice to live heaven on earth or hell on earth. We can choose light or darkness. We can choose to be in a state of joy and bliss, just the same as we can choose to live in a state of misery and pain. The beauty about this is that we always have a choice and no choice is right or wrong, good or bad. It just IS. And if we surrender to what is and are able to release our own judgment, we are able to fully receive whatever lesson or gift is there for us. And there is always a gift. It's up to you whether you want to resist it or receive it. We must surrender and let go of our agendas to receive what the Universe has to give us in each moment, especially in our darkest moments. We must allow ourselves to go through whatever we need to go through without shame or judgement. We must fall in love with the contrast and surrender to the will of the Universe or God or whatever it is you believe in. We must be immensely grateful for our light and our darkness.

> *"Light and Darkness. One cannot exist without the other." —Luis Marques*

Just as we are to accept the light and dark within ourselves, we must also do the same with others. After all, no one is perfect. When you are able to accept and embrace others just as they are, it is a huge indicator that you also love and embrace yourself. We project how we feel inside out into the world. This is why, in order to heal your relationships and create the connection that you desire with others, you must first heal the relationship that you have with yourself.

Empathy and compassion are key traits of a magnetically confident person. Empathy is sort of like the gateway to compassion. It is the ability to feel what someone else is feeling by imagining how it might feel for you to be in their shoes—it is a method of relating. Compassion, on the other hand, is about action. It is the willingness to support someone through their emotional suffering. The Latin root of compassion means "to suffer with." When you practice compassion, you are not running away from the suffering or pretending it doesn't exist. It is the ability to be present and provide whatever support the person needs in that moment. In many cases, the simple act of listening intently and hearing the other person out is all that they need. Other times, they may need more than that. In those cases, you'll just want make sure you are honoring your boundaries while you are honoring their needs.

Practicing empathy and compassion is a beautiful thing. It is what creates harmony, connection, love, and oneness in this world. It also requires you to not take things other people feel, say, or do personally. You may have heard the saying, "hurt people, hurt people." Trust me, I know having compassion for others can be easier said than done at times, especially when someone manages to trigger the sh*^ out of you! It can be tempting to bite back and tell them to "F*ck off with your crazy projections and pure potent BS!" I get it. But honey, you are a magnetically confident and classy person and "ya'll don't say that!"

(BTW, that is my favorite scene from Step Brothers). As Anne Lamott so gracefully puts it, "It is better to be kind than to be right."

There was a time when I fought with my mom incessantly. I mean, you couldn't leave us in a room for more than a few hours before we would either start bickering or screaming at each other's throats. I have this one vivid memory, which makes me chuckle right now as I'm envisioning it, where my mother literally chased me around the house, huffing and puffing, yelling, and waving a remote in her hand for a solid ten minutes. I laugh about this now because I've gone through major transformative processes that have allowed me to see beyond those events and to the truth of the matter. It definitely wasn't funny at the time!

Look, my relationship with my mom wasn't and still isn't perfect. I don't believe any relationship is. However, a big reason we fought so much was because of the resistance I had built up toward her and the perspective I was choosing to have toward our relationship. I refused to have empathy or compassion and instead, I was just so adamant about *being right*. There is always a cost that comes with being right. In this case, it was costing me my relationship with a woman who I loved dearly and meant the world to me—my mom. During my transformational journey, I did a lot of deep work around this. I realized many, many eye-opening things but probably the two most valuable lessons I learned that allowed me to totally transform my relationship with my mom into the beautiful, healthy, close, and loving relationship I have with her today is:

1. I was choosing to be in a constant state of resistance toward my mother and the nature of our relationship because I was so focused on what I didn't like about it versus what I love. You attract more of what you focus on.

2. I realized that my mom was loving me the best way she knew how. The second point just brought me to tears as I wrote it. My mom was not raised in the most loving environment. Growing up, her mother was the overly-critical, harsh type that showed her love and affection in her own less-direct ways and her father wasn't very present. I look at my mom today and see a divine, beautiful, and loving soul. I love her with all of my heart. I see the little girl that felt neglected, unloved, and not good enough in her childhood and I love her too. I am so grateful for our relationship and that I am now able to see and embrace her for the incredible mother that she is.

Chapter Challenge:

Releasing Resentment

Think of someone you currently have or have had resistance or resentment toward in the past. This could be someone you just don't get along with, or someone that hurt you. Close your eyes, focus in on the image of this person and see them as a little girl or little boy. Imagine the hurt they may have experienced in their lives. Surround them with white light and allow yourself to have compassion for them. Believe that they are honestly doing the best they know how. Feel a sense of gratitude for them and the role they play or have played in your life. After all, everything that happens has a purpose and sometimes our greatest lessons come from the most painful teachers.

Allow yourself to connect, forgive and let go of the resentment. Notice the difference you feel in your body after doing this. Holding on to resentment toward others weighs us down and keeps us stuck in the past, using up energy we could be allocating to the present moment. When you choose to forgive and release resentment, you are letting go of the negative energy that is weighing you down and keeping you from being at your best. You are taking back your power and sending a message into the Universe that you are are, also, worth forgiving.

Transform
pain to purpose
self-pity to
self-power
victim to victor.

OWNERSHIP & RESPONSIBILITY

"You attract what you are, not what you want. So if you want it then reflect it!" —Tony Gaskins

A magnetically confident person does not blame other people, things, or outside circumstances for their present condition. She knows and understands that she is the cause and the source for everything that shows up in her life: the good, the bad, the pretty, the ugly...all of it. With that knowing, she draws in the power to attract and choose the people, circumstances, and situations that are in her life. By the same token, a person who lacks in self-confidence believes they are essentially doomed to a certain fate or circumstance because of some weird, unknown force that they believe they have no control over, usually referred to as "bad luck." It is this belief itself that creates and perpetuates their reality.

This is the difference between being in ownership and responsibility versus being in victimhood.

This is such a crucial component to magnetic confidence that I cannot stress enough. When you believe you are responsible for everything that happens around you, you instantly become confident and powerful. The opposite is true when you are being a victim. Think about it. When you place blame on your circumstances, situations, or other people, you are giving your power away to those things. You are sending the message out into the Universe that you are powerless.

Instead, take it on. Take back your power and be in ownership of the situations you are in, the results you've sourced, and how you feel about them. A magnetically confident person does not permit victimhood. They do not allow themselves to fall prey to unfavorable situations or circumstances because they know that they have *the God-given ability to choose how to respond to everything*. They know that they have the power to turn things around; to go from victim to victor. They turn pain into purpose and pity into power. It is all a conscious *choice* that they can make at any given moment. Yep, you too have been blessed with the gift and the freedom of choice. It's a beautiful thing. In every moment, in every situation, you have the choice of how to respond.

Growing up, my dad really emphasized this idea of ownership with me. He taught me to always be responsible for my feelings and internal state. If I was ever feeling frustrated, angry, or sad, he would remind me that I was *choosing* that and nothing or no one could make me feel that way but myself.

Have you ever said something like, "She is stressing me out!" or "This is making me so frustrated!" or "He makes me so mad?" Here's the essential issue with each of these statements: you are making it about THEM instead of YOU.

You are placing blame on and giving your power away to the person or situation. No one can make you do anything. Do not let your internal condition be determined by your external condition. That is dangerous and risky. Plus, it deems you powerless! And you are not powerless, my love. You have been blessed with the eternal power of choice. And not just one choice...but many, many choices.

So, the next time you catch yourself saying that someone or something is "making" you feel or act a certain way, let's add in a little reminder phrase that will help you draw your power back and get you set on the path to attracting what it is you really want to experience. You are going to add in the phrase: "I am choosing to allow" before your blame statement! So it would look something like this: "*I am choosing to allow Tiffany to make me upset.*" This puts you back in control. It reminds you that you are choosing your experience and that you have the power to choose something different that actually serves you.

I remember the first time I used the lesson my dad taught me against him. We still laugh about it today. I must have been about ten years old. I did something bad (though I can't remember what it was) and my dad was really upset. We were arguing in my room when he said, "Ashley! You're making me so mad!" to which I calmly replied, "No, no dad...only YOU can make yourself mad." Obviously, my dad had nothing to say to that and walked off grumbling "Damnit, she's right" under his breath. *Insert devilish grin here*

Magnetically confident people do not give their power away to circumstances, situations, or others. They don't allow themselves to be identified with anything outside of themselves. They stay true to who they are and what they want. They don't settle, and they certainly don't just sit and let life happen to them. They are not a passenger, but the driver of their life and they know that whatever direction, destination, or obstacle they encounter is ultimately up to them.

While it is true that you cannot always control what happens outside of you, you can always control what is inside of you and how you respond to external circumstances. If you are ever in an undesirable situation and for some reason are having trouble thinking of choices you can make, here are three choices that you always have in every situation:

1. **LEAVE IT**

   Exit. Go. Walk away! You are not a prisoner and you're not being held captive. You always have the freedom to leave any undesirable situation or state.

2. **CHANGE IT**

   Do something about it! Think of what you want to create and make it happen. Focus on your ability to cause, create, and influence change.

3. **REFRAME IT**

   Turn it around and flip your perception to something that serves you. You can learn to love and accept the reality you are in by simply changing the way you view your present situation. Everything is perception!

> Touch it, bring it, pay it, watch it,
> Turn it, leave it, stop, format it.
>
> Technologic...Technologic...

Sorry...I did it again. I think in songs.

I received a message the other day from a girl who really, really wanted to play on a softball team but didn't like the energy of many of the girls that were on the team. Softball is her passion and she really wanted to play. Her question to me was "Should I join the team and subject myself to the negative energy of those girls or just not play softball this season?" So, looking at our three choices that we always have in these kinds of situations, she can either choose not to be a part of it (and miss the opportunity to do what she loves), use her influence and power to create a new energy dynamic between the girls, or learn to look at the situation through another lens that serves her.

In this case, my vote was for option two or three, while powerfully reminding her that it is ultimately *her* choice. For example, instead of looking at the situation as an unfavorable one where she is "subjecting" herself to these girls, she can look at it as a favorable situation where she gets to do what she loves. She can also *choose whether or not to allow* the other girls to affect her internal condition of joy and happiness while she plays.

Responsibility vs. Taking Things Personally

> *"Don't take anything personally. Nothing others do is because of you. What others say and do is a projection of their own reality, their own dream. When you are immune to the opinions and actions of others, you won't be the victim of needless suffering."* —Miguel Ruiz

There is a difference between being in ownership and taking things personally, and the difference is in your level of attachment. When we are in ownership and holding ourselves as responsible for an unfavorable outcome or event, we have almost no emotional attachment to it. The outcome is simply neutral feedback for us. It is a learning experience, nothing more. We do not allow it to change or dictate who we are or what we stand for. However, when we take things personally, we are attaching our well-being and self-identity to the outcome or result. We are allowing our inner state and our self-confidence to be reliant on external factors. While it is always important to pay attention to and be in ownership of your results, it is not healthy to let them define you. YOU are not your results. Your results are a byproduct of you and your choices. While you may have sourced and created them, they do not create you.

You must release personal attachment to other people, objects, events, and situations. You must surrender and be open to receiving the lesson or gift of growth that is there for you. And when I say surrender, I don't mean actually giving up or becoming dormant. What I mean by surrender is to simply *let go*. Let go of attachment and anything that is not serving you in these moments. And yes, sometimes this might mean letting go of control. Other times, it may mean letting go of what was or could have been and embracing what is.

Taking things personally is exactly that—*taking*. Each time you take something personally, you are taking from yourself and from others. When you are in ownership without attachment, you are giving to yourself and to others. You are giving yourself power and giving others compassion and respect.

The difference between being in ownership and taking things personally is a very, very powerful distinction. It will truly free you in so many ways once you realize and practice it.

The only
way out is
through.

FACE THE UGLY

"The only way out is through." —Robert Frost

So many of us are so stuck on the how-to. We want to be told what to do and how to do it. The part most are missing, and frankly avoiding, is what is in the way. Why haven't you gotten that promotion yet? Why are you working in a job that you hate? Why haven't you attracted the man of your dreams yet? Why do you suck at public speaking? Why do you continue to overeat? Why do you not have the kind of friendships you want to have?

What is in the gap between where you are now and where you want to be? What is in the gap between who you are now and who you want to be?

It's so much easier not to think about these things and bypass "what's in the way" altogether. Most of us just don't want to go there. It's easier not to go there. We don't want to face the ugly because it's uncomfortable and, quite frankly, it's scary and it can hurt. So, let's just talk about the good-feeling comfortable stuff like the how-tos and the possibilities! Okay sure, you can do that. But before we embark on this how-to journey, we must find out what's in the way. We must own and embrace all parts of us: the good, the bad, the ugly. We must confront our self-limiting beliefs and barriers that hold us back. The more we avoid and resist them, the more power they have over us.

"What we resist, persists." —Carl Jung

And it doesn't just persist, it grows. It festers. It prevents us from moving forward and creating meaningful, sustainable change. We've got to get real so we can get moving!

The best way to find out what is in the way for you is to pay attention to the next time you feel yourself avoiding or resisting something. You will feel it in your body. It will feel uncomfortable and you might even get an icky, dry taste in your mouth. As soon as you find yourself in this place, acknowledge that you are in resistance. Just identifying this will be a powerful pattern-interrupt for you. From there, take inquiry. Get curious. Ask yourself why you feel uncomfortable? What is that little voice in the back of your head telling you right now? What are you afraid might happen? What is your fear?

You may not come up with answers to these questions right away, but the point is to allow yourself to engage with something you may have previously completely avoided. It is about mustering the courage to confront something that feels uncomfortable. Allow yourself to go there. Give yourself permission to feel whatever it is you need to feel. Confront it, don't avoid it, and don't resist it. The only way out is through. It may feel painful, but remember that feelings are only temporary. You will move through it and you will come out on the other side.

I used to get this really horrible, uncomfortable anxious feeling whenever I would have to go to any kind of networking or social event. Even events where you are just sitting and listening, like conferences, gave me anxiety because I knew there would be a break or point where everyone would get up and start socializing. Some may call it social anxiety. So, what did I do? I avoided all such events and situations as often as I could. I remember being at events where, at some point, the facilitator would tee up a partner activity (where you find a random partner and engage in some kind of structured or unstructured dialogue). As soon as he started explaining the process, I would start to feel extremely anxious and nervous, so I would sneak out of the room and stay hidden in the bathroom until I was sure it was over.

The truth is, avoiding was only making things worse and I just became more and more socially anxious. When I finally stopped avoiding, took inquiry, and got real with myself, I realized what was really going on. My urge to escape was almost unbearable, but I stuck it out. I paid close attention to what that little voice inside my head was saying as I gave myself permission to feel all the anxious, nervous, uncomfortable feels. It's almost as if I was my curious-self watching my anxious-self go through everything. I was watching, experiencing, and feeling all at once.

I promised I'd keep it real with you guys, so I'm going to let you in on what was going on inside my head and the internal dialogue that took place. The short version goes a little something like this:

> *I am afraid that they won't like me. I am afraid I won't know what to say and I will make them feel awkward. Oh god, what if I do or say something really awkward? What if they figure me out?! They will know I don't belong here! They will know I'm not one of them and that I'm an outsider. I'm better off just eating lunch in the bathroom stall than facing that kind of rejection!*

Now, I'm not going to lie to you and say none of those things ever happened the first few times I made myself confront what I used to avoid. Because, as the law of attraction says, negative attracts negative. What you focus on is what you get. It takes practice. Once you realize the internal dialogue that's taking place, you can dismantle and shift it. You can separate what's real from what's not. For example, while it may be true that you feel anxious, is it really true that they will reject you? How can you know for sure? The feeling of anxiety is a reality. I felt anxious.

Being rejected? That's a fear. It hasn't happened yet. It's not reality, it's imaginary.

False

Evidence

Appearing

Real

Once you identify what is truth and what is fear, you get curious. Ask yourself these three questions about the fear-based thoughts and conversations you are having in your head that hold you back:

1. Where does it come from?

2. Why am I choosing to go there now?

3. What is it costing me and is it worth it?

Chances are that there was a traumatic experience, typically from early childhood, that thoughts and beliefs like "I don't belong here" or "I'm not good enough," or "They won't like me" come from. Most of our core beliefs were formed during childhood and it is said by many researchers that our entire belief systems are pretty well-formed by the age of six and our belief systems are essentially how we interpret life. They are the lenses we are looking through and the filters by which we process incoming information, people, and situations as we move our way through life.[3]

So, step one is asking yourself where it came from. What happened to make you believe you don't belong? What happened to make you believe you would be rejected? For me, it was the painful experiences of rejection I faced in my childhood. Now it's time for you to get real with you. What happened?

Once you are able to identify where the self-sabotaging thoughts come from, you can check in with reality by acknowledging that:

1. Yes, that happened.

2. It's not happening anymore and it doesn't have to!

Being aware of where our limiting beliefs and conversations stem from is very powerful because it allows us to separate the experience from who we are so we no longer identify ourselves with it. Instead, we identify it for the experience that it was and realize that it does not define who we actually are and what we are capable of.

Next, you ask yourself why you still choose to go there even when you know it's not actually true. Believe me, even after you realize where it came from and gain that awareness, you will likely still choose to go there again—whether consciously or subconsciously. You are human after all. I still do it. It will show up and try to disguise itself in new, different forms. Sometimes we will be able to identify, dismantle, and shift quickly, while other times we may fall prey to old patterns. There is no right or wrong, there is only resisting or growing. As long as you don't resist the reality that you chose to go there, you can use it as an opportunity to further grow yourself.

When you realize where the negative, self-sabotaging thoughts come from and still choose to go there, you are probably getting something out of it. There's something in it for you. However, it is inauthentic and 100% fear based. It is a false benefit. There is almost always some false, hidden benefit we get for continuing to indulge in self-sabotaging thoughts and behaviors.

When I would avoid social settings, I got to stay in my comfort zone and be right about the belief that I didn't belong and that I wasn't worthy of acceptance, love, or belonging. I got to be right that I was alone, because I was perpetually isolating myself. I got to be right that "nobody will like me" because I didn't even show up or give them the chance. How could they possibly like me? I had created my own self-fulfilling prophecy.

As you can see, all of these were completely false benefits and they sabotaged my ability to experience true connection, love, and happiness. When you can see and identify them as false benefits, you will be able to clearly see that they are not actually benefits at all. Quite the opposite. They are costs. These self-sabotaging beliefs are costing you relationships, joy, prosperity, connection, success, health, and the list goes on.

So now, the final question: is it worth it?

One of my good friends and mentors, Lori Taylor once told me a story about her and her horse, Payday. Lori and Payday have always had a very special bond and she always says that he teaches her so many valuable lessons about herself and about life in general. While Payday is an incredibly talented and beautiful horse, he also has his not-so-pretty moments. One day, Lori was riding him and they were practicing jumps when he tripped and nearly fell. When Lori tried to pull him up, her spurs hit him really hard, which startled him. He took off running before she was fully back on the saddle and slammed her into a wall. Lori ended up breaking her T3 and suffered major PTSD from the whole experience. It was physically and emotionally traumatizing for her. From that point forward, Lori carried this fear almost every time she rode Payday. It was a limiting belief that she created from the accident: *I'm not safe*. This took the joy away from riding Payday, as she was always so focused on the fear of getting hurt again. Her trainer started noticing the difference in Lori's energy when she would ride Payday and confronted Lori about it. What Lori discovered through a powerful coaching session with her trainer is that in the 120 times she has ridden Payday, she has gotten hurt twice. Which means that 2% of the time, Payday is not rideable. That also means that 98% of the time, he is amazing and exhibits exceptional performance. Lori was trading 98% of her joy of riding Payday for a 2% chance of getting hurt. When she realized this, she looked her fear and sabotaging belief in the face and said, *not worth it!*

Why give up on a lifetime of joy, bliss, love, and connection because we experienced a brief period of pain? Is trading 98% of profound joy for a 2% chance of pain really worth it? The odds really are in your favor and the Universe really does have your back. It's time to move forward. You got this.

Chapter Challenge:
Switch It Up!

*Starting tomorrow (or today if you are reading this in the wee hours of the morning), you are going to try doing everyday things a little differently. Okay, very differently. This is meant to be a fun, yet insightful challenge so let go and allow yourself have fun with it!

*Whether the change you make is big or small, make a change to the way you do things on an hour-to-hour or even minute-by-minute basis. Challenge yourself!

*The whole point of this is to get out of your comfort zone, shake things up a bit, and recalibrate your reality. Pay attention to how you feel before, during, and after you do things differently. Be open to what new perspectives or insights may surface.

*Here are some fun examples of things you can do differently. The goal is to do as many as you can in one day!

» Brush your teeth with the opposite hand.

» Part your hair on the opposite side.

» Take a different route to work.

- » If you shower facing the shower head, turn around and try it the other way.
- » Text with the opposite hand (at least once).
- » Use all new emojis you've never used before. The entire day.
- » Sleep on the opposite side of the bed.
- » Write with your opposite hand (at least once).
- » Get your nails painted a color you would never normally choose.

So many options to choose from! The more you can accomplish in twenty-four hours' time, the better!

The purpose of this exercise is to start getting you comfortable with feeling uncomfortable. The biggest growth happens outside of your comfort zone.

The only way to
overcome darkness
is to shine light
on it.

AUTHENTICITY

"Let go of who you think you should be in order to be who you are. Be imperfect and have compassion for yourself." —Brene Brown

Growing up, I was sort of awkward looking and definitely on the more dorky side. I remember the first time my peers actually started liking me and accepting me. My looks had blossomed sometime between high school and college. Finally, I wasn't so awkward and I actually started fitting my peers' standards of beauty. I was finally "accepted" because of my looks. I actually remember a girl coming up to me and blatantly saying, "You're pretty. We should be friends," in college. I mean, how much more surface-level can you get?

Not-so-surprisingly, I ended up placing almost all of my value in my outward appearance. I would cling to this surface-level approval and validation that I was getting from others to make me feel like I was worth the friendship, love, and connection that I really craved. I depended on my looks to get what I wanted and anytime it didn't work, whatever was left of my self-esteem would take a huge hit. I was living a totally surface life, I was completely inauthentic, I had no real confidence, and I was severely unhappy. My confidence relied on external factors, what other people thought of me.

When your confidence is reliant on something outside of you, whether it be being liked, receiving compliments, attention, money, fame, awards, or any other form of external validation, that is not real, authentic confidence. You are relying on external conditions to create your internal condition. It is external identification, identifying with a temporary, external condition rather than your internal, eternal self.

True, radiant, and magnetic confidence happens from the inside out and it is unconditional. It is a deep knowing that you are worthy, you matter, and your voice matters. It is a deep acceptance of who you authentically are and a strong stand for what you authentically want.

Courage

> *"Courage starts with showing up and letting ourselves be seen."* —Brene Brown

> *"It takes courage to grow up and become who you really are."* —E.E. Cummings

Authenticity is having the courage to be yourself. It is showing up as the real, raw you, no matter where you are or who you are with. This is absolutely essential to creating magnetic confidence. Authenticity is honestly one of the most, if not *the most* attractive quality one can possess. And quite frankly, it is refreshing in today's world.

Look, I'm definitely a fan of social media. Thanks to social networks like Facebook and Instagram, we have the ability to connect at mass scale and share our messages with hundreds, thousands, or even millions of people at the press of a button. Sometimes I'll sit and think "How did we ever *not* have social media?" However, just like everything else in this world, it has a shadow. The dark side of social media is the pressure to be perfect and fit these false images of perfection. With all of these swipe rights and swipe lefts, people are so quick to judge. There are all of these unrealistic expectations around what you should be and what you should look like. This can be damaging and downright depressing. It is also breeding more and more "digital clones", followers who try to be just like the person they follow on social media instead of being themselves.

Judgment & Rejection

For as long as I can remember, I longed for acceptance. I just wanted to feel like I truly belonged. There was a point in my life when I was so desperate for acceptance that I pretzeled into whatever or whoever I needed to be in order to be accepted and liked. I was a chameleon. I did whatever I needed to do to fit in and belong. Meanwhile, I was losing sight of who I really was. I would have these bouts of depression that would last days at a time. I remember feeling this overwhelming sense of shame because I knew how fake I was being but didn't have the courage to stop and just be myself. I was so scared of being judged, rejected, or worse, found out for the fraud that I was.

Living in this misalignment with my authentic self was exhausting and it certainly didn't feel good. I mean, sure I would get these temporary moments of gratification when someone would give me that nod of approval or laugh at one of my jokes, but at the end of the day I was drained and unhappy. It is exhausting trying to be someone other than who you are.

The fact is this: if you feel you have to try and mold or pretzel yourself into something that you're not just to fit in and be accepted or liked by others then clearly *you are not accepting of and do not like yourself.* It all comes back to self-love and self-acceptance. Chances are, you are running some serious "not enough" conversations in your head, whether consciously or subconsciously.

I'm not pretty enough.

I'm not smart enough.

I'm not funny enough.

I'm not _____ enough.

Yep, that was me. Lots of "not enoughs." I didn't love myself enough to be myself. I was constantly judging myself and I wasn't accepting who I really was. But here's the kicker: *how could I possibly expect others to love and accept me if I didn't even love and accept myself?* I was living a self-fulfilling prophecy.

So, here's the deal. If judgment and not being liked are real fears for you and you find it hard to be yourself, here are two facts that will help you confront that fear head on and set you free from them so that you can move courageously forward and be unforgivably and authentically YOU.

1. <u>People will judge.</u> They are human, after all, and it is human nature to judge. So, just know that you will be judged. Probably not as often as you think you will, but it will happen at one point or another.

2. <u>There is no such thing as being liked by everyone</u>. There is always a hater. There is always someone who won't agree with you. This is the beauty of diversity and perception!

Why am I saying that these two facts will set you free? Because they are the truth. The minute we stop battling with reality and just accept the truth at face value, we will instantly feel a sense of relief and inner peace because we are no longer resisting what is. Now, I'm not saying that everyone is going to judge you or that no one will like you. I am merely shedding light on the darkness here and the only way to overcome darkness is to shine light on it.

The interesting thing about judgment and rejection is that they are, in most cases, just a reflection of our own insecurities. We tend to judge others based on what we believe is acceptable and we judge ourselves by that same criteria. We essentially project our judgment fears onto others. When you fear someone is judging you, what you are really doing in that moment is judging yourself and the other person. So, if it makes you feel better, just know that when people judge you, it is about them, not you. Have compassion for the person who is judging or rejecting you. Just imagine how much they must be judging and rejecting themselves.

Stop rejecting yourself and others will stop rejecting you. The more you fear that no one will like you for who you are, the less you will be who you are and the less of a chance people will even be given the opportunity to know who you are! The fear will become your reality. You will create a self-fulfilling prophecy like I did.

So, how do you create radiant, magnetic authenticity? You must have the courage to risk being judged and rejected. You must stand in the face of your fears. As Oprah Winfrey says, "Courage is feeling the fear and doing it anyway." You must also completely detach yourself from the judgments people place on you and any act of rejection you are faced with. You cannot let it affect the way you view yourself. At the end of the day, you are with you. You may not belong with them, but you will always belong with you. So what if Sally Shanahan doesn't agree with your point of view or if Bobby Bologna thinks your jokes are as stale as eight-week-old bread. Girl, you do you. Be unforgivably you. Nothing is more attractive than someone who knows who they are, what they want, and doesn't waiver at the thought of what others might think about them! Now, *that* is magnetic confidence.

Chapter Challenge:

Being and Attracting

*Grab a pen and paper and write down everything that you want in a romantic partner, whether you are single, in a relationship, or married.

*Focus on ways of being and put them in "he is" or "she is" form. For example:

- » He is compassionate
- » He is kind
- » He is loyal
- » He is generous
- » He is humble

...etc.

*Once you have identified and written down ten ways of being that you desire in your romantic partner, go through each of the items on the list and cross out the words "he is"/"she is" and write "I am."

*In order to attract what we want in another, we must first be it ourselves. We are what we attract and we attract what we are.

*Go through each item on your list that now says "I am" and rate yourself a 1-5 (5 = Yes, I have mastered this way of being. 1 = No, I get to work on this!). Be honest and sincere, no one is going to see this but you. Those that you rated a 4 or above, you will have no problem attracting these ways of being in another, as long as you truly are being those things. Any that you rated a 3 or less, you really get to focus in and work on these if you want to attract them in another person. You must first become and embody what it is that you desire and watch as you begin attracting more of it to you.

Your tribe is a reflection of you.

CHOOSING YOUR TRIBE

If you consistently feel uncomfortable or anxious around a certain person or group of people, that is a big indicator that you are not being yourself. In those moments, it is important to tune in and tap back into the authentic you. Maybe it's not that you necessarily feel uncomfortable or anxious, but that you really just don't like a lot of the people you are surrounded with. Maybe there is something about them that really bothers you and you just wish they were different. Well, I hate to break it to you babe, but you're the one that needs to be different! If you are attracting people that aren't in alignment with who you are or who you want to be, then you are also not aligned with who you are or who you want to be. In other words, you are not being true to yourself. Your vibe attracts your tribe! The law of attraction says like attracts like. Fake people will likely attract other fake people, just like authentic people will attract other authentic people. That's just how it works.

If you are unsure about how you may be perceived by others or whether you are truly being authentic, take a look at the people you most frequently surround yourself with. They are a reflection of you. For example, if you frequently find yourself in unpleasant circumstances and situations, or surrounded by unhappy, negative, or toxic people, you may want to flip the focus here. Get curious about how you could be causing, creating, or manifesting these people in your life. There is something about you that is attracting those kinds of people, situations, and circumstances into your life.

It is crazy what a transformation I have had with my tribe in just two years' time. I used to hang out with very surface-level people, because I was surface, and frequently subjected myself to very low-vibrating activities, such as gossiping, which I participated in to be cool and accepted. Fast forward to now and I have an incredible high-vibing tribe of powerful, genuine, and authentic women who I love with all my heart! We have weekly girls' nights (well, more like bi-weekly) and every time I leave our girls' nights I feel like I'm floating on a cloud! I'm filled with so much joy and gratitude for these amazing friendships and women that I've managed to magnetize into my life.

Authenticity is magnetic because it is not just admirable, it also instills a sense of trustworthiness in others. If you are acting fake, people will see you as just that: an act. Would you trust someone who you felt was being fake and putting on an act? We are energetic beings. We can feel fake energy right away and decide what to do with it. Most of the time, the natural human response is not to trust it. People trust people who are true to themselves. Odds are, if you are true to you, you will likely be true to others.

Unapologetically Shameless Living

Have you ever blurted out "Sorry!" when you collide with someone on the street? Do you apologize for things that don't even really make sense to apologize for? A really good girlfriend of mine used to consistently do this. It was almost as if, by some crazy impulse, she felt the incessant need to blurt "I'm sorry" for everything. If she stumbled on her words, "I'm sorry!" If she coughed, "I'm sorry!" If she sneezed, "I'm sorry!" If she moved, "I'm sorry!" She would reactively utter an apology for everything she did or didn't do, even if she literally did nothing wrong. One day, I approached her about this...and she immediately apologized. Lol. I'm kidding. Actually, she might have. Anyway, I brought it up and she looked a bit confused at first. She didn't even realize how much she was saying it! She was almost completely unaware of how much she was apologizing for herself. She was operating on autopilot. It was her automatic response to say "I'm sorry" anytime she felt the least bit uncomfortable. While this may seem like an innocent habit, it is actually an indicator of low self-worth. Constantly over-apologizing sends a signal to the Universe that you are sorry for your existence. It completely undermines your ability to magnetize and attract what you want into your life. While apologizing can certainly be a powerful tool for resolving conflict and building trust, it is also vital that you view yourself as worthy to make your way in the world. Today, I am proud to report that my overly-apologetic girlfriend is now walking with confidence, worth, and conviction and she's #sorrynotsorry!

One of my favorite bloggers, Maya Washington, otherwise known as "Shameless Maya" is a beautiful and stunning example of shameless authenticity. She started her YouTube channel back in 2012 as a social experiment to see what would happen if she documented herself being completely shameless and raw for a year straight. She was totally transparent and real with her followers, sharing about her divorce and other vulnerable topics. Well, it's safe to say her courageous experiment turned out to be an incredible success. Her bravery and courage to be seen exactly for who is without a shred of shame wasn't just refreshing and inspiring, it was *magnetizing*. She now has millions of followers and subscribers from around the world and has collaborated with big name brands such as Target, CoverGirl, Google Store, and many more. And it all started when she decided to follow her heart, be shameless, and boldly step into the light.

A magnetically confident person acts and speaks with conviction and certainty. Her words and actions are aligned with her beliefs and her character. She lives a congruent life. She is in harmony. She is unapologetically herself, flaws and all. She is free, authentic, and has the courage to be seen. She is shameless.

Growing up, you may have been told to be quiet. You may have been shamed for expressing yourself, wearing certain clothes, or saying certain things. You being told those things or judged that way was never about you, it was about them. And SO WHAT! So what if you make someone uncomfortable or intimidated? Girl, *do* YOU! Or, as Shameless Maya would say, "Do you, boo!" Do what lights you up. Be what you feel like being. Live however you want to live. Don't let anyone ever dim your light or dull your sparkle. Because, let's be real, that is not why you were put on this planet. You are one in 7.4 billion. You are a diamond and you are meant to shine!

One of my absolute favorite quotes in the entire world is by Marianne Williamson. Really let what she says sink in for you. Allow yourself to see how you could be dimming your light, playing small, or selling yourself short of your true potential.

> *"Our deepest fear is not that we are inadequate. Our deepest fear is that we are powerful beyond measure. It is our light, not our darkness that most frightens us. We ask ourselves, who am I to be brilliant, gorgeous, talented, fabulous? Actually, who are you not to be? You are a child of God. Your playing small does not serve the world. There is nothing enlightened about shrinking so that other people won't feel insecure around you. We are all meant to shine, as children do. We were born to make manifest the glory of God that is within us. It's not just in some of us; it's in everyone. And as we let our*

own light shine, we unconsciously give other people permission to do the same. As we are liberated from our own fear, our presence automatically liberates others." —Marianne Williamson

When you let your light shine, you inspire others to do the same. When we give ourselves permission to be wildly free and authentic, just our presence and energy alone will give others permission to do the same. So, next time you think about dimming that light of yours for the sake of someone else, know that even though you may think you are being gracious, you are actually taking from them in that moment. Your light has the capacity to give the gift of light to others. Dimming your light robs others of receiving this gift, and likely many others. Plus, if we bring magnetism and the law of attraction back into play, dimming our light and downplaying our accomplishments will not attract more to us.

When is the last time that you celebrated, I mean really celebrated, an accomplishment? Given the opportunity, many of us are quick to beat ourselves up for a silly mistake but we rarely take the time to celebrate our victories and triumphs. I'm especially talking to you over-achievers reading this right now. Celebrating your achievements and victories not only builds up your self-confidence, it also attracts more achievements and victories to you. So, celebrate away! Celebrate EVERYTHING. Acknowledge all your wins, big or small, and express gratitude for all of your gifts because you have many.

In all this talk about celebrating, shining our light, being unapologetic, and in ownership of all of our results,

I want to draw a thin line in the sand. A magnetically confident person knows the difference between owning and boasting, between shining and flaunting, between celebrating and bragging, and between cockiness and confidence. That difference is *graciousness*. One gives while the other takes. One comes from wholeheartedness while the other comes from insecurity and ill-will.

A magnetically confident person is always gracious about her victories, triumphs, knowledge, and possessions. She uses them to give to others, not take from them. She inspires others through her achievements. When she shines her light, she shines with the pure, genuine intention to make a positive impact on the world around her. When she shines, she inspires others to shine, too.

Chapter Challenge:
Courage Cards

*Think of five courageous acts you've accomplished in the past. These are challenges you've overcome and achievements you've made in the face of your fears, moments of courage.

*Write them down. Read and repeat them out loud a minimum of three times.

*Now, in your mind's eye, visualize five cards. Each card is going to represent each of your moments of courage. Imprint each of your courage cards in your mind and store them away somewhere safe and accessible.

*From this point forward, in any moment where you feel the onset of fear or anxiety, you can pull out your deck of courage cards to give you a quick bravery boost. You'll look at each of those courageous accomplishments and think, "Wow, if I was able to do that, then I can certainly do this!"

This challenge was inspired by one of the amazing, intelligent, and powerful women in my tribe who is a best-selling author, certified coach, and public speaker, Jessica Leigh. Love you, girl!

Live in the the
here and now.
The greatest
presents are in
the present.

BEING PRESENT

"The present moment is the only moment available to us, and it is the door to all moments." —Thich Nhat Hanh

"Wherever you are—be all there." —Jim Elliott

I used to have a serious issue with remembering people's names. Whenever I would meet someone for the first time, I would forget their name almost instantly after they introduced themselves. It was like it went in one ear and out the other. I maybe remembered around 5-10% of people's names. I sort of just accepted this as my reality and was convinced I had some sort of incurable name memory disorder. Well, this all changed when I had a very uncomfortable, painful experience during a personal development training. I had spent almost two weeks with a team of around thirty people. We were together for sometimes twelve hours straight, days at a time. It was super intimate. We shared vulnerable details of our lives and created very deep bonds with each other. Well, one day, out of nowhere, I was put in a situation where I needed to address every person in my group by their first name. Yep, you guessed it. I barely remembered any of them. Out of the thirty individuals that I had become so intimately close with, I remembered six of their names. There was even a girl that, *just minutes* before the activity, had shared something extremely vulnerable with me that brought both her and I to tears—and I didn't remember her name. It was my worst nightmare. Even just writing and looking back this experience makes me want to cry. I don't know if I have ever been more horrified, ashamed, or uncomfortable in my entire life.

As Bryant McGill says, "Whatever makes you uncomfortable is your biggest opportunity for growth." This was a huge growth moment for me and what I uncovered from this forever changed my life. I had no name memory disorder. That seemed to be the issue on the surface, but it was not the *real* issue. The real issue was that I was so in my head, insecure, and worried about how I was being perceived by others that I was not being present. Whenever I would meet people for the first time and we would introduce ourselves, I was so focused on myself and making a good first impression that I was completely disconnected and not present with the person I was meeting. I was in the past or the future, worrying what they thought or are going to think about me. I mean, how could I really hear and remember a person's name if my mind was somewhere else? No wonder their name was going in one ear and out the other! Of course, this all ties back to an even deeper issue that is really the issue under all issues: *self-worth and self-love.*

A magnetically confident person is fully present because she knows her worth and does not allow herself to be bothered by anxiety of the past or future. She lives her life in the here and now. She realizes deeply that the present moment is the only moment that truly matters because it is the only moment she has.

> *"Realize deeply that the present moment is all you have. Make the Now the primary focus of your life."*
> —Eckhart Tolle

When you are present, you are respecting yourself and others. Being present and connected in your conversations with others makes them feel heard. It says, "You are important and special." And remember, you reflect what you are. Presence is an incredibly attractive, magnetic, and powerful quality of a confident person.

Shake It Off

> *"All problems are illusions of the mind."*
> —Eckhart Tolle

Have you ever found yourself sitting in a funk for hours, or even days, at a time? Do you have trouble accepting and moving on from unfavorable situations or events that involve embarrassment, pain, or heartbreak? Do you tend to sit in self-beat-up for prolonged periods of time after you make mistakes? Do you often find yourself feeling stuck in a state of unhappiness, frustration, anger, or depression? I can relate to all of these. This was my life. The skill I was lacking, that is also a huge indicator of low self-esteem and self-confidence, was the ability to *shift*.

I cannot emphasize the power of shifting enough and how drastically it will transform your life as you master it. When you are able to shift out of an undesirable state, you become that much more powerful. You are realizing that you are the one in charge of your internal condition and that you have a choice of how long you want to stay in an undesirable state. This is probably one of the most valuable and admirable traits of a magnetically confident person. You will get better and better at shifting, the more you practice it.

So, next time you find yourself in an undesirable state, ask yourself this: *"How long do I want to stay here?"* and answer honestly. My answer has ranged anywhere from, "I don't" to "ten minutes" to "all day." The point in asking yourself this is to:

1. Create a pattern-interrupt and pull you into consciousness.

2. Really honor yourself and own power to choose.

Just knowing that you, and only you, can answer that question is enough for you to take your power back and bring you back up from whatever is getting you down.

At the end of the day, your capacity to shift is really dependent on the level of love you have for yourself and how worthy you believe you are of attaining a desirable state. Yes, once again, it comes back to self-love and self-worth. You just can't escape it. Sorry, not sorry! Be kind and compassionate with yourself and know this is your journey. There is no such thing as being transformed. Transformation is an ongoing, infinite adventure. There is always going to be a next level of growth for you. Always. As long as you are on the path toward enlightenment, self-love, and worthiness, then you are golden, my love. Know that every journey looks different and sometimes life throws curve balls. At the end of the day, the more you love and accept who you are and own your worth, the better you will become at not letting anything outside of you affect who you are and your mission on this planet.

Magnetic confidence is not something you strive to have by doing, doing, doing, and more doing. It is a way of *being*. It is you. It who you choose to be in each moment. It is when you choose to be authentic, vulnerable, and courageous. It is when you choose to deeply love and accept yourself. It is when you own your power and your voice. It is when you realize that you are worthy, that you have a divine purpose on this planet, and you matter.

NOW WHAT?

Now that you've read my book, there are many things you can do to continue down the path of self-growth and being the best, most confident version of you. Remember, an investment in yourself is the best investment you can possibly make because YOU are the source of everything in your life now and what you will attract moving forward. It all starts with YOU.

Suggested Reading

I absolutely LOVE reading. I read every single day as part of my morning ritual. Whether it's for 10 minutes or 45 minutes, I always create time. I mostly read books centered around mindset and personal growth. I believe reading these kinds of messages first thing in the morning is a super powerful way to start the day and it sets me on the right trajectory. Here are some of my favorite books.

Hey! Also, if you're on Instagram, I'm always updating my "Books" highlight on my page @ashley.hann. I usually read 1-2 books per month, so you can keep up with me there!

- » *The Power of Now* by Eckhart Tolle
- » *The Mastery of Love* by Don Miguel Ruiz
- » *The Four Agreements* by Don Miguel Ruiz
- » *The Universe has your Back* by Gabrielle Bernstein
- » *Loving What Is* by Byron Katie
- » *Switch on your Brain* by Dr. Caroline Leaf
- » *Feeling is the Secret* by Neville Goddard
- » *Braving the Wilderness* by Brené Brown
- » *The Gifts of Imperfection* by Brené Brown
- » *Think and Grow Rich* by Napoleon Hill
- » *NLP: The Essential Guide to Neuro-Linguistic Programming* by NLP Comprehensive and Tom Dotz
- » *I Am That Girl* by Alexis Jones

In-Person Trainings and Workshops

Reading only goes so far. If you really want to create radical transformation, you must roll-up your sleeves and DO THE WORK. As I mentioned, I've been to many workshops and seminars. What stimulated the most radical part of my growth and transformation was a ~4-month long intensive training I did called Ascension Leadership Academy hosted in San Diego. There are many courses like this located around the country. I highly recommend investing in training like this. YOU come above everything else and YOU deserve it! Here are a few options that I trust and recommend in order of personal preference:

- » Ascension Leadership Academy (San Diego, CA) - www.alasandiego.com
- » Heart Core Leadership (San Diego, CA) - www.heartcoreleadership.com
- » Mastery In Transformational Training (Los Angeles) - www.mittraining.com
- » Next Level Trainings (Columbus, OH) - www.nextleveltrainings.com
- » Choice Center (Las Vegas) - www.choicecenter.com

Remember, **you are worth the investment.**

ONE LAST THING…

If you enjoyed this book or found it at all useful, it would mean so much to me if you'd post a review on Amazon or recommend it to family and friends. **Your support truly makes a difference** and it's the reason I continue to push and create. **YOU inspire me**. I love reading your feedback and getting to know each and every one of you!

> To leave a review, visit the link provided below:
> https://tinyurl.com/MagneticConfidence

Thank you so much for your support!

BIBLIOGRAPHY

1. Lipton, Bruce H. *The Biology of Belief: Unleashing the Power of Consciousness, Matter & Miracles.* Carlsbad, CA: Hay House, Inc., 2014.

2. "The Many Faces of Perfectionism" Monitor on Psychology. Accessed March 05, 2018. http://www.apa.org/monitor/nov03/manyfaces.aspx.

3. "So What Exactly is a Belief System?" So what exactly is a belief system. Accessed February 26, 2018. http://www.takechargecounseling. org/yahoo_site_admin/assets/docs/Article_2_-_ What_Is_A_Belief_System.326110726.htm.

Connect with Ashley

Instagram: @ashley.hann

Facebook: @itsashleyhann

YouTube: 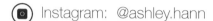 @ashleyhann

Twitter: @itsashleyhann

Learn more at
www.AshleyHann.com

I'd love to hear from you!

contact@ashleyhann.com